D1091269

Eyewitness Accounts of the American Revolution

Diary of
Lieut.
Anthony Allaire

The New York Times & Arno Press

Diary of Lieut. Anthony Allaire

Diary of Lieut. Anthony Allaire,

OF FERGUSON'S CORPS.

MEMORANDUM OF OCCURRENCES DURING THE CAMPAIGN OF 1780.

Sunday, March 5th. The following corps marched from Savannah, viz.: Light Infantry, commanded by Maj. Graham; American Volunteers, Lieut. Col. Ferguson; New York Volunteers, Lieut. Col. Turnbull; North Carolinians, Lieut. Col. Hamilton; South Carolinians, Col. Innes; Dismounted Legion, Maj. Cochrane; one company of Georgia Dragoons, Capt. Campbell; and the First Battalion of the Seventy-first regiment, Maj. McArthur—in number about fifteen hundred.

We marched from Savannah at six o'clock in the morning; arrived at Cherokee Hill, nine miles from Savannah, at twelve o'clock, and encamped to refresh ourselves. At three o'clock in the afternoon got in motion, and marched to Abercorn, eight miles from Cherokee Hill; here we encamped and lay all night. Disagreeable, rainy weather.

Monday, 6th. At eight o'clock we got in motion, and marched to Ebenezer, a village situated on Savannah river, eight miles above Abercorn. It contains about twenty houses and a church. The inhabitants are high Dutch. It is garrisoned by our troops; there are four redoubts, but no cannon in any of them.

Tuesday, 7th. Remained at Ebenezer. Pleasant morning, showery evening and very warm. Spent part of the evening with two Indian Captains, John and James; smoked tobacco and drank grog with those two devils incarnate.

Wednesday, 8th. Still remained at Ebenezer. Orders to draw two days' provisions, and be ready to march at reveille beating. Several men taken suddenly ill with pain and swelling of the extremities, occasioned by a weed that poisons where it touches the naked skin, when the dew is on it.

Thursday, 9th. The army got in motion ; passed a causeway three-quarters of a mile in length, overflowed with water from two to three feet deep. We marched to a plantation ten miles from Ebenezer, called the Two Sisters, situated on Savannah river. It was formerly a public ferry ; but at present nobody lives at it. The houses are destroyed.

Friday, 10th. The American Volunteers and British Legion marched three miles up the Augusta road to Tuckasse-King. Here we encamped, and took breakfast at ten o'clock in the morning. A Rebel Lieut. Johnson with twenty men surrounded a poor man's house here this morning. They heard we were in motion, but not being certain of it, they came to find out the truth. They did no damage to the family ; neither did they tarry long, being informed that we were in possession of the Two Sisters, they thought it proper for the brothers to take themselves off. This is the first Rebel party we have heard of. At three o'clock in the afternoon received orders to take the ground we left in the morning, where I and part of the detachment lay all night. One division crossed the river—the others to follow as expeditiously as possible.

Saturday, 11th. Crossed the Savannah river ; such a fresh that the boats were brought through woods a mile and a half ; the water was from four to ten feet deep, where in a dry time we might have marched on dry ground. The horses were swum over the river—the current sets down very rapid.

South Carolina, Sunday, 12th. Lay encamped a quarter of a mile from the river in the field where Gen. Moultrie was encamped last summer when our troops were retreating from Charleston. A foraging party of the Dragoons fell in with some Rebel Light Horse ; and Mr. Campbell of the Georgia Dragoons received a slight wound.

Monday, 13th. The American Volunteers and British Legion were ordered forward twenty-six miles, to secure the passes of Bee creek, Coosawhatchie and Tullyfinny Bridge, which we effected. This day passed Turkey Hill, a pleasant country seat belonging to one Mr. Middleton. We took up our ground at dusk, at Coosawhatchie Bridge, where the Rebels opposed our troops last May and got defeated. A cool, pleasant day for marching.

Tuesday, 14th. Found several horses, a quantity of furniture, Continental stores and ammunition, hid in a swamp by one John Stafford, a sort of Rebel commissary who lives at Coosawhatchie, and is, by the by, a cursed fool, which alone prevents his being a d——d rogue. About five o'clock in the afternoon we crossed Tullyfinny Bridge, and proceeded about six miles to Mr. McPherson's. Fifty of the militia on horseback had just left this plantation and gone to John McPherson's. A small party of ours pursued them, but could not come up with them, Maj. Cochrane with the Legion were in pursuit of another party of Rebels on another road ; but being mis-piloted, he arrived just before break of day in front of our picket. He immediately conjectured we were the party he had been in pursuit of all night. He halted and made a position with an intent to attack as soon as it began to be clearly light ; but the alertness of our sentinels obliged them to come on sooner than they intended. He immediately, on their firing, rushed on the picket; they gave the alarm, but were driven to the house, where our men ready for the attack, expecting it was Rebels, a smart skirmish ensued. The sad mistake was soon discovered, but not before two brave soldiers of the American Volunteers, and one of the Legion were killed, and several on both sides badly wounded. Col. Ferguson got wounded in the arm by a bayonet, Lieut. McPherson, of the Legion, in the arm and hand.

Wednesday, 15th. Still remained at McPherson's plantation ; foraging parties get everything necessary for the army.

Thursday, 16th. Remained at McPherson's plantation, living on the fat of the land, the soldiers every side of us roasting turkeys, fowls, pigs, etc., every night in great plenty ; this Mr. McPherson being a great Rebel, and a man of vast property, at present in Charlestown. About thirty Rebels showed themselves this morning, a mile and a half in front of us. A party went out in pursuit of them ; but returned without effecting anything—the jockeys being on horseback easily made off.

Friday. Still at McPherson's. Three militia men were brought in prisoners by a scouting party of the American Volunteers, and a number of horses. Received orders to march to-morrow morning.

Saturday, 18th. Marched from McPherson's plantation to Saltketcher, a Rebel party consisting of eighty mititia, commanded by a Maj. Ladson, placed themselves on the north side of the river to oppose our crossing. They were amused by a company of the Legion returning their fire across the river at the place where the bridge formerly was, whilst the Light Infantry and remainder of the Legion crossed the river below, and came in the rear of them before they were aware of it. Here the bayonet was introduced so effectually that a Capt. Mills, and sixteen privates of the Rebels, could not exist any longer, and of course gave up the cause. Four were badly wounded, and one taken prisoner that luckily escaped the bayonet. Maj. Graham, of the Light Infantry, and Maj. Wright, of the Georgia Loyalists, slightly wounded. The former continued to command his battalion, and the latter continued his march. Two privates of the Light Infantry were also slightly wounded. We remained all night at Ogilvies' plantation, on the side of the river called Indian land. This day's march was very tedious—a disagreeable, rainy, cold day, and through a swamp where the water was from two to three feet deep.

Sunday, 19th. Passed Saltketcher river—where the bridge formerly stood, but has been destroyed since the rebellion—in boats, and swam the horses. The causeway on both sides of the river is overflowed with water from two to three feet deep, at the ferry house, about a quarter of a mile from the river. Dr. Johnson dressed the wounds of Maj. Wright and the four Rebels that were bayoneted yesterday. Marched one mile and a half to a tavern kept by Mr. Gibson, who is at present prisoner in Charleston, for not taking up arms when his country so loudly calls for assistance.

Monday, 20th. The army got in motion, marching about two miles. Received orders to halt, the rear guard being fired on; it proved to be the York Volunteers, getting the boats on the carriages at the river, were fired on by a skulking party of rascals on the other side of the stream. Three poor lads of the York Volunteers were killed. What damage was done to the Rebels we are not certain. Detained by this and repairing of bridges on the road, we only marched seven miles this day. Took up our ground at a place called Godfrey's savannah.

Tuesday, 21st. The army got in motion. Marched to Fish Pond river. Here we were detained to repair the bridge till evening. Before we crossed we moved on about three miles, through a swamp, over an exceeding bad causeway. This day Col. Tarleton, with his dragoons, joined us from Beaufort, where he had been to get horses—his being all lost on the passage from New York. We took up our ground about ten o'clock at night, and remained till ten o'clock next morning.

Wednesday, 22d. The army got in motion at ten in the morning, and marched as far as Horse Shoe, where we again were detained to repair the bridge. After crossing, continued our march to Jacksonsburgh, a village containing about sixty houses, situated on Pon Pon, or Edisto river. The most of the houses are very good; the people tolerable well to live; some large store houses for rice, from which they convey it by water to Charleston market. In short, it is a pleasant little place, and well situated for trade, but the inhabitants are all Rebels—not a man remaining in the town, except two, one of whom was so sick he could not get out of bed, and the other a doctor, who had the name of a friend to Government. The women were treated very tenderly, and with the utmost civility, notwithstanding their husbands were out in arms against us.

Thursday, 23d. All the army, except the Seventy-first regiment, and greatest part of the baggage, crossed the river in boats and flats, the bridge being destroyed. Col. Tarleton came up with a party of Rebel militia dragoons, soon after crossing the river at Gov. Bee's plantation. He killed ten, and took four prisoners. Gov. Bee was formerly Lieut. Gov. under His Majesty, is now one of the members of Congress, and Lieut. Gov. of South Carolina.

Friday, 24th. The remainder of the baggage and Seventy-first regiment passed Pon Pon river. The army got in motion about one o'clock in the afternoon, and marched about seven miles, where we halted all night. A flag of truce, consisting of a Capt. Saunders, Capt. Wilkinson, one private and a servant, came in at the rear of the army. Just as we halted they were severely reprimanded by Gen. Paterson for their unmilitary conduct. He told them that they were ignorant of the profession they followed ; and in consequence of their behavior he must detain them all night, and, as to their request, it would not be granted, which was likewise very unmilitary, it being to speak with the prisoners and give them some necessaries. The gentry of the flag were led blindfold to their lodging. This day Col. Ferguson got the rear guard in order to do his King and country justice, by protecting friends, and widows, and destroying Rebel property ; also to collect live stock for the use of the army, all of which we effect as we go, by destroying furniture, breaking windows, etc., taking all their horned cattle, horses, mules, sheep, fowls, etc., and their negroes to drive them. We had a disagreeable night— very heavy shower, with a great deal of heavy thunder and lightning.

Saturday, 25th. The army got in motion at reveille beating, and marched to Stono, where was formerly a bridge, called Wallace's Bridge. We took up our ground about three o'clock in the afternoon, where we remained all night. Light Infantry and part of the Dragoons went over the river.

Sunday, 26th. Consumed the whole day in passing the baggage and live stock over the river, the bridge that formerly stood here being destroyed, and the one just made very bad. We took up our ground as soon as we got over, on a neck of land that runs down between Stono and Rantowle's, only one mile between the two rivers. This day the Commander-in-chief came to us from James Island, which is six miles distant.

Monday, 27th. Two companies of Light Infantry, American Volunteers, and one company of Dragoons, crossed at Rantowle's in scows; the rest of the army crossed yesterday. Col. Hamilton, of the North Carolinians, and Dr. Smith, of the Hospital, proceeding about a mile in front of the army, to Gov. Rutledge's house, were immediately surrounded by three hundred Continental Light Horse, and they consequently made prisoners. The British Dragoons fell in with them soon after, and had a skirmish ; the Rebels soon gave way, and showed them the road, as is customary for them to do. Qr. Master Sergeant McIntosh, of the Georgia Dragoons, badly wounded in the face by a broadsword. Several Dragoons of the Legion were wounded. How many of the Rebels got hurt we can't learn ; but they did not keep up the combat long enough for many to receive damage. This morning, Capt. Saunders, that came in with the flag on the 24th, was sent out; his attendant, Capt. Wilkinson, not being mentioned in the body of the flag, is detained as a prisoner of war. We took up our ground on Gov. Rutledge's plantation, about one mile from his house, where we remained all night.

Tuesday, 28th. The army got in motion about nine o'clock in the morning, and marched to Ashley Ferry, where we met the British and Hessians, Grenadiers, Light Infantry and Yagers, under command of Sir H. Clinton. We continued our march down the river about six miles to Lining's plantation; it is situated on Ashley river, nearly opposite Charlestown, and commands an extensive view towards the sea.

Wednesday, 29th. Sir Henry Clinton, with the British and Hessians, Grenadiers, Light Infantry and Yagers, passed over Ashley river to Charleston Neck, early in the morning. Spent the day in viewing Charleston and found it not a little like New York; for Ashley and Cooper rivers form a bay exactly like East and North river at New York.

Thursday, 30th. Incessant firing of small arms on the neck ; cannon at short intervals. This firing was at the Commander-in-chief and his family reconnoitring. He forbid the British returning the fire. Lord Cathness, standing by the side of Gen. Clinton, was shot through the body by a musket ball; one Yager killed.

Friday, 31st. Engineers' tools, etc., carried over from Lining's Landing, and broke ground without molestation, under direction of Maj. Moncrieff. Rode two miles to see two redoubts, one of which has six, and the other two thirty-two pounders in them, at the mouth of Wapoo-Cut, a river that runs from Stono to Ashley river, and separates from the main land what is called James Island. Those two redoubts are exactly opposite Charleston.

Saturday, April 1st. Some cannon and mortars moved over Ashley river from Lining's Landing.

Sunday, 2d. Rode down to view our fleet that lay at Stono.

Monday, 3d. Marched to Ashley Ferry to cover the Dragoons of the Legion whilst crossing the river. Marched from this up the river to Henry Middleton's plantation ; passed several famous country seats, one called Drayton's Hall, belonging to William Henry Drayton, deceased, who was a member of Congress, and died at Philadelphia. Constant firing at our works from the Rebels all day.

Tuesday, 4th. Constant cannonade from the Rebels, both from their batteries and shipping; one of their ships, endeavoring to move up Cooper river, was fired on from our works, and drove back.

Wednesday, 5th. Constant cannonade from the Rebels at our works on the Neck, in the evening. Our batteries at the mouth of Wapoo-Cut opened, and kept up a warm fire for a few minutes, then the firing ceased on both sides.

Thursday, 6th. Cannonade from the Rebels all day by intervals. In the evening our batteries opened on the Neck, and at Wapoo-Cut fired all night by intervals.

Friday, 7th. Cannonade at intervals as usual,

Saturday, 8th. But little firing from the Rebels. Rainy, disagreeable morning. The Rebels were reinforced with thirteen hundred men
last night, commanded by a Gen. Scott. They fired a *feu de joie*, and
rang all the bells in town on the occasion. About four o'clock this
afternoon the fleet hove in sight, coming up under full sail with a fresh
breeze at south west, and passed Fort Moultrie—the Rebel fort that
they boasted of on Sullivan's Island, which no fleet could ever pass.
They were but a few minutes passing. What damage is sustained we
have not yet learned. The Richmond lost her fore top-mast; a cutter
lay opposite the fort all the time the fleet was passing, with a flag hoisted
to point out the channel. A heavy cannonade from the Rebels'
batteries, which the shipping returned as they passed with a spirit
becoming Britons.

Sunday, 9th. Admiral Arbuthnot came on shore, and went over to
Head-quarters on the Neck. By him we were informed that there were
only seven men killed, and fifteen wounded, in passing Sullivan's Island.
The shipping damage was so trifling that 'twas not worth mentioning.

Monday, 10th. Nothing extraordinary. Cannonade from our batteries during the night to cover the working parties.

Tuesday, 11th. Col. Ferguson came from Head-quarters. Informs
us that the town was summoned to surrender to his Britannic Majesty.
Answer was returned, that they thought it necessary as well as their duty
to defend it to the last extremity, which they meant to do.

Wednesday, 12th. Received orders to march. The North Carolinians were ordered to join Col. Ferguson. We left Lining's plantation
about seven o'clock in the evening, and marched to Bacon's Bridge,
twenty-two miles, where we arrived at five o'clock on Thursday morning;
very much fatigued. We halted to refresh till seven. Cool weather.

Thursday, 13th. Got in motion at seven o'clock in the morning.
Marched through a small village called Dorchester. It contains about
forty houses and a church. Continued our march to Middleton's plantation at Goose creek, about fifteen miles from Bacon's Bridge, and ten
from Dorchester. Here we met the Legion about one o'clock in the
afternoon, and halted till ten at night. Then, in company with them,
got in motion and marched eighteen miles to Monk's Corner, being
informed that Col. Washington's, Pulaski's, Bland's, and Horry's Light
Horse lay here. We arrived just as day began to appear on Friday
morning, and found the above enemy here, in number about four hundred, including some militia that arrived the day before, commanded by
Gen. Huger. Luckily for them, they were under marching orders, which
made them more alert, when the alarm was given, than usual, which
alone prevented their being all taken completely by surprise. They
made off with great expedition. We pursued, overtook and killed

Pulaski's Major Vernier, wounded a French Lieut. Beaulait,* and one other officer; about sixty privates were taken, fifteen or twenty of whom were wounded. We had but one man wounded, and he very slightly. We took thirty wagons, with four horses in each. A number of very fine horses that belonged to their troops were likewise taken, and converted to British Light horses. Col. Washington and all their officers made but a narrow escape; their baggage, letters, and some of their commissions were taken.

Friday, 14th. Remained at Monk's Corner, collecting the stores, etc. About seven o'clock at night, accidentally a store house caught fire, in which were two casks of powder; was very much alarmed by the explosion, and all got under arms. This confusion was scarcely over when three ladies came to our camp in great distress : Lady Colleton, Miss Betsy Giles, and Miss Jean Russell. They had been most shockingly abused by a plundering villain. Lady Colleton badly cut in the hand by a broadsword, and bruised very much. After my friend, Dr. Johnson, dressed her hand, he, with an officer and twelve men, went to the plantation, about one mile from camp, to protect Mrs. Fayssoux, whom this infamous villain had likewise abused in the same manner. There he found a most accomplished, amiable lady in the greatest distress imaginable. After he took a little blood from her she was more composed, and next morning come to camp to testify against the cursed villain that abused them in this horrid manner. He was secured and sent to Head-quarters for trial.

Saturday, 15th. The army got in motion about twelve o'clock. My friend, Dr Johnson, and myself had the happiness of escorting the ladies to their plantation. Before we got there we were met by a servant informing us that there were more plunderers in the house. This news so shocked Lady Colleton and Mrs. Fayssoux, who were some distance before us, and the young ladies in a carriage, that I am not able to describe their melancholy situation, which was truly deplorable. After their fright was a little over we passed on to their house ; but the ladies fearing to stay alone, Lady Colleton and Mrs. Fayssoux got into the carriage, Miss Giles behind me, and Miss Russell on a horse, which I led for fear he should make off with my fair one ; they passed on with us four miles to a plantation called Mulberry Broughton, and here we bid adieu to our fair companions with great regret, they thinking themselves out of danger of any insults. We this day countermarched to the twenty-three mile house, and halted all night.

Sunday, 16th. Got in motion about three o'clock in the morning,

---

* Beaulait has been very unfortunate since in America He received seven wounds by a broadsword, in a charge of Campbell's Light Horse, when Charlestown was besieged by Gen. Provost, and two at Monk's Corner, which amounts to nine, four or five of them in the face.—A. A.

and marched to Strawberry Ferry, a branch of Cooper river. Took up the day in passing the army and baggage over the stream. After crossing, marched four miles to Bono Ferry, another branch of Cooper river, where we came up with the baggage of the Thirty-third and Sixty-fourth Regiments, and of the Legion. Here we lay all night, as it took up the night to get this baggage over the river. A Captain's guard from our detachment was sent over to take charge of a store house full of household furniture, brought out of town and deposited at a Maj. Butler's for safety—the store was full of very rich furniture of all kinds.

Monday, 17th. Crossed Bono Ferry and passed on to Miller's Bridge, over a branch of Wando river, where we took up our ground about nine o'clock in the evening. This day passed St. Thomas' church, where we met the Thirty-third regiment.

Tuesday, 18th. Began to fortify at the Bridge, and make a block house in order to keep post here with a few men.

Wednesday, 19th. Maj. Ferguson, with fifty of the American Volunteers, and part of the North Carolinians, moved on to join the Thirty-third and Sixty-fourth regiments, and the British Legion, which had gone forward to attack a Rebel post at Lempriere's Point. The British were coming back; they had marched up to the fort, but found it so strong that it was imprudent to storm it with so few men.

Thursday, 20th. Remained at Miller's Bridge, finishing the block house. Col. Tarleton surprised and took nine sloops with goods, stores, etc., and twenty pieces of cannon.

Friday, 21st. Capt. Ryerson, with forty American Volunteers, a subaltern, and twenty of the Thirty-third, and a subaltern, and twenty of the Sixty-fourth regiments, remained at Miller's Bridge to defend and keep the pass. The remainder of the Thirty-third and Sixty-fourth regiments, American Volunteers, and British Legion, counter-marched twelve miles and took up our ground at St. Thomas' church.

Saturday, 22d. Took possession of the parish house; took up and was under the disagreeable neccessity of detaining a lady of the town, on suspicion of her being a spy.

January 23d. Moved from the house into the woods for the convenience of shade—very warm weather.

Monday, 24th. Lord Cornwallis joined us and took command. About ten o'clock in the evening there was the most tremendous cannonade I ever heard, and an incessant fire of musketry. The Rebels sallied out and took eight of the Light Infantry prisoners, upon which the whole line got under arms; some in their hurry getting out without putting on their coats, were taken by the others for Rebels, and fired on, which unluckily occasioned warm work for a few minutes. Sixty odd of ours got killed and wounded by our own men. The Rebels were repulsed, and they finding their muskets rather an incumbrance threw thirty odd of them away.

Tuesday, 25th. About eight o'clock in the morning got in motion ; were joined by the Twenty-third regiment and Volunteers of Ireland. We proceeded on, passed over Miller's Bridge and Waputa Bridge, took possession of Waputa meeting house, about seven o'clock in the evening, where we halted till two in the morning.

Wednesday, 26th. At two o'clock in the morning got in motion, and marched seventeen miles to Mount Pleasant, opposite Charleston, where we took possession of the ground, on which the Rebels had one eighteen pounder. Here is a ferry from this to a town called Hibban's· Ferry ; there are very good barracks here if finished, that were begun before the rebellion. Sullivan's Island is about a half a mile distant from the Point. There is a bridge from the Point to the Island with four arches. The barracks were used for a hospital, in which we took some invalids and a doctor. About six miles from the Point stands Christ Church. This night I might properly sing, "Content with our hard fate, my boys," on the cold ground where I lay—wrapt up in my great coat, with my saddle for a pillow. A blustering cold night.

Thursday, 27th. Got in motion about one o'clock in the morning, and countermarched to Waputa meeting house. Cold north-east wind.

Friday, 28th. Fortified the small house by the side of the meeting house, at ten o'clock at night. Intelligence being received that the Rebels had left the fort at Lempriere's Point, and gone to Charleston, we got in motion and marched down to discover the fact. We arrived about four in the morning, and found the fort occupied by the Navy, a Lieutenant of the Navy, commanding officer. The Rebels were gone to Charleston.

Saturday, 29th. Countermarched to our old grounds at the meeting house. Pleasant weather.

Sunday, 30th. Got in motion at three o'clock in the morning, in company with the York Volunteers, and marched to Lempriere's Point to take post there. We got to our ground about seven o'clock in the evening, where we found four eighteen, two four pounders, and five swivels, that the Rebels left in their fort. A very disagreeable post it is, being nothing but a bank of sand, where, in a windy day, you must keep your eyes shut or have them filled with sand. Here used to be a ferry called Lempriere's Ferry.

Monday, May 1st. Bathed in Wando river.

Tuesday, 2d. Began to fortify Lempriere's Point. Maj. Ferguson, with a detachment of American Volunteers, marched down to Mount Pleasant, stormed and took possession of a little redoubt, located partly on the main, and partly on the bridge that leads to Fort Moultrie. This cuts off the communication from Sullivan's Island, and keeps them on their proper allowance. The Rebels ran off from the redoubt, though it was very strongly situated, after they fired about a dozen shot.

Wednesday, 3d. Still fortifying Lempriere's Point. In the evening began a cannonade on the neck, which continued very heavy all night— an incessant firing of musketry, the cannon chiefly from the Rebels, small arms from us. This night took their hospital ship that lay opposite the town.

Thursday, 4th. Continued fortifying the Point. Rode from Lempriere's Point to Mount Pleasant; dined with Capt. Ord, of the Navy. After dinner rode to Hurdle's [Haddrell's?] Point to view the redoubt which Col. Ferguson stormed the second of May, with only sixty men and never was more surprised in my life, for twenty men like the American Volunteers would have defied all Washington's Army.

Friday, 5th. Very windy—in danger of losing one's eyes by the blowing of sand. Cold blustering night.

Saturday, 6th. Very disagreeable, windy day. Still at Lempriere's. News just received from Lord Cornwallis, that Lieut. Nash and eleven dragoons that were patrolling, were taken by Washington and Horry's Light Horse near Santee river. Col. Tarleton was immediately ordered to pursue them. He overtook them at the river; charged and killed a number, and took a Major and thirty privates. The patrolling party that had been taken were in a boat, rowing across the river. Upon their seeing Col. Tarleton, they immediately seized the guard, threw them overboard, rowed themselves back and joined their regiment again. Col. Washington and Horry took to the river and swam across it.

Sunday, 7th. Orders to get ready to march with two days' provision, at a minute's notice. Maj. Ferguson had obtained permission to attack Fort Moultrie. He rode forward with four dragoons to reconnoitre· We were to remain at our post till we got orders for marching. The first news we heard was the fort was in possession of the British; the Rebels had surrendered themselves prisoners of war. Capitulation was as follows: Capt. Hudson of the Navy summoned the fort on Friday, and received for answer: "Tol, lol, de rol, lol: Fort Moultrie will be defended to the last extremity." On Saturday he sent another flag, and demanded a surrender, acquainting Col. Scott that the Lieutenant with the flag would wait a quarter of an hour for an answer. If the fort was not given up, he would immediately storm it, and put all the garrison to the sword. At this Col. Scott changed the tune of his song, begging that there might be a cessation of arms, that the fort would be given up on the following conditions: that the officers both Continental and militia, should march out with the honors of war, and be allowed to wear their side arms; the officers and soldiers of the militia have paroles to go to their respective homes, and remain peaceably till exchanged; and the continental soldiers to be treated tenderly. Granted by Capt. Hudson. About eight o'clock Sunday morning, Colonel Scott with his men, about one hundred and twenty, marched out of the fort, piled

their arms, Capt. Hudson marched in, took possession of Fort Moultrie, the key to Charleston harbor; which puts it in our power to keep out any forcing enemy that would wish to give the Rebels any assistance. Taken in the fort, fifty barrels of powder, forty-four pieces of cannon, one brass ten inch mortar, three thousand cannon cartridges, five hundred ten inch shells, forty thousand musket cartridges, three month's salt provision, a lot of rice, forty head black cattle, sixty sheep, twenty goats, forty fat hogs, six wagons, two stand of colors, an amazing quantity of lunt;* and, in short, so many other articles which are
. * Match-cord for firing cannon.
necessary in a fort that it would take me a week to set them down.

Monday, 8th. Six o'clock in the morning, Sir Henry Clinton sent in a flag, and demanded the surrender of Charleston. General Lincoln requested cessation of hostilities till eight o'clock—from eight to twelve; and the truce continued until four o'clock Tuesday evening when Sir Henry Clinton receiving a very insolent request, sent in word that he plainly saw that Gen. Lincoln did not mean to give up the town; that the firing should commence at eight o'clock in the evening, at which time began a most tremendous cannonade, throwing of carcases and shells into the town, and an incessant fire of musketry all night.

Wednesday, 10th. Firing still continued all day, and very brisk all night.

Thursday, 11th. The town set on fire by a carcase, which burnt several houses. The Rebels sent out a flag soon after; our firing continued without taking notice of their flag. They showed the second flag, which we accepted. It was begging the terms that had been offered the last truce. Sir Henry Clinton answered them the firing should cease until he could send and consult Admiral Arbuthnot. The terms were granted.

Friday, 12th. The gates were opened, Gen. Leslie at the head of the British Grenadiers, Seventh, Sixty-third and Sixty-fourth regiments, and Hessian Grenadiers marched in, and took possession of Charleston, and soon leveled the thirteen stripes with the dust, and displayed the British standard on their ramparts. Still at Lempriere's.

Saturday, 13th. Remained at Lempriere's.

Sunday, 14th. Went to Charleston to view their strong works. Saw the poor Rebel dogs very much chagrined at not being allowed to wear their side arms.

Monday, 15th. Magazine blew up—set the town on fire—burnt several houses. Capt. Collins and Lieut. Gordon, of the artillery, Lieut. M'Leod of the Forty-second regiment, and about thirty privates, perished by the explosion. In what way the accident happened is not certain; 'tis supposed by throwing the captured arms into the magazine, one went off, and set fire to the powder.

Tuesday, 16th. The American Volunteers relieved the Navy, and took command of Fort Moultrie.

Wednesday, 17th. Spent the day in writing letters for New York. Nothing new.

Thursday, 18th, to Sunday, 21st. Lay at Fort Moultrie. Nothing extra.

Monday, 22d. Received orders for marching—went to Charleston.

Tuesday, 23d. About three o'clock in the afternoon returned in a six-oared boat, and had the pleasing view of sixty or seventy large ships coming into the harbor.

Wednesday, 24th. Lay at Fort Moultrie.

Thursday, 25th. The detachment was relieved by British and Hessian Grenadiers. The American Volunteers marched up to Mount Pleasant, and crossed over to Charleston. Marched through the town, and took up their ground just in front of the lines. The horses and baggage with myself crossed from Lempriere's Point to the Ship Yard, which is about two miles from the town.

Friday, 26th. The following corps got in motion about three o'clock in the morning, under the command of Col. Balfour, of the Twenty-third regiment, viz—Light Infantry, commanded by Maj. Graham, three companies of the Seventh by Capt. Peacock, American Volunteers by Maj. Ferguson, and the Prince of Wales American Volunteers by Lieut.-Col. Patterson—in number about six hundred. Marched out to the Ten Mile House, and halted. Made bough houses to cover the men from the heat of the sun. Heavy thunder shower.

Saturday, 27th. Marched at five o'clock in the morning; passed through a piece of low ground covered with magnolias in full bloom, which emitted a most delicious odor. We took up our ground at a plantation about two miles from the Twenty-Three Mile House.

Sunday, 28th. Got in motion at two o'clock in the morning. Marched to Monk's Corner and halted. Dr. Johnson and myself went and dined with Lady Colleton, Miss Russell and Miss Giles, the ladies we protected in their distress when we were here the fourteenth of April.

Monday, 29th. Lay encamped in a wood at Monk's Corner. Spent an agreeable afternoon at Lady Colleton's, with Miss Russell and Miss Giles.

Tuesday, 30th. Got in motion at five o'clock in the morning, and marched to Gen. Moultrie's plantation, at a place called Prussia, where we halted.

Wednesday, 31st. Got in motion at half past four in the morning; marched to Greenland swamp, and halted.

Thursday, June 1st. Got in motion at five o'clock in the morning, and marched to Nelson's Ferry, Santee river. By express were informed that Col. Tarleton, Monday, the 29th, fell in with a body of Rebels.

[Buford's corps] forty miles above Camden. He summoned them to surrender—received an insolent answer, charged them, killed one Lieutenant-Colonel, three Captains, eight Subalterns, one Adjutant, one Quarter-Master, and ninety-nine Sergeants and rank and file. Wounded three Captains, five Subalterns, and one hundred and forty-two rank and file. Made prisoners two Captains, one Subaltern, fifty rank and file. Total killed, wounded and taken prisoners, one Lieutenant-Colonel, eight Captains, fourteen Subalterns, one Adjutant, one Quarter-Master, and two hundred and ninety-one Sergeants, rank and file; three stand of colors taken, two brass six-pounders, two howitzers, two wagons with ammunition, one artillery forge wagon, fifty-five barrels powder, twenty-six wagons loaded with clothing, camp equipage, musket-cartridges, cartridge-boxes, flints, etc., etc. Killed of the Legion, Lieut. McDonald and Ensign Campbell, serving with the cavalry, two privates of the cavalry, and one of the Light Infantry. Total, two Subalterns, and three rank and file. Wounded Lieut. Patterson, seven dragoons, making eight rank and file of the cavalry, and three of the infantry. Total wounded, one Subaltern, and eleven rank and file.

Friday, 2d. Lay encamped in a pleasant field near Nelson's Ferry. Ordered to be in readiness to march at two o'clock in the morning.

Saturday, 3d. Got in motion two o'clock in the morning. Marched to Campbell's plantation, where we halted in the woods for the convenience of shade. This place is seventy-seven miles from Charleston.

Sunday, 4th. Lay in the woods at Campbell's plantation. Some prize wine shared to the different corps; very convenient time to drink his Majesty's health.

Monday, 5th. Got in motion at two o'clock in the morning, and marched to Cave Hall, St. Matthew's parish. Just below our camp was a remarkably large cave, about an hundred feet deep. There is a room formed by a rock sixty feet long, and forty wide, with famous grand arches formed by nature. Through the middle runs a beautiful stream of water, which heads in a fountain at the farther end of the cave. This day twenty militia men came in, and brought the new-fangled Governor of Georgia prisoner. He was sent to Charleston. He had taken protection from Lord Cornwallis as a private man.

Tuesday, 6th. Got in motion at three o'clock in the morning, and marched thirteeen miles to Col. Thomson's, and halted on the march. Started two bucks; they ran in amongst the men. One of them got caught. The militia were in from all quarters.

Wednesday, 7th. Lay encamped at Col. Thomson's plantation; a field in our rear covered with sensitive plant and passion flower.

Thursday, 8th. Still at Thomson's plantation. A thunder shower every afternoon.

Friday, 9th. Encamped still at Thomson's plantation; wrote a letter to Miss ——.

Saturday, 10th. Got in motion and left Thomson's at twelve o'clock at night, and marched eighteen miles to Beaver creek, where we halted. Maj. Graham, and two flank companies of the Prince of Wales American Volunteers, remained at Thomson's. This day a company of militia came in with their arms. A Henry Meholm, an old man eighty-one years of age, this day met us; he had left home with an intention to go to Charleston, and had walked upwards of an hundred miles when he met us. His errand was to get some kind of assistance. He had been plundered by the Rebels, and stripped of everything. What is remarkable, this old gentleman left at home a child between two and three years old.

Sunday, 11th. Got in motion at five o'clock in the morning, and marched five miles and halted.

Monday, 12th. Got in motion at two o'clock in the morning, and marched fourteen miles to Congaree Stores. This day passed a plantation where were about four hundred acres of Indian corn growing—the property of one man.

Tuesday, 13th. Lay at Congaree Stores. Many good friends to Government have suffered much by the Rebels.

Wednesday, 14th. Lay at Congaree Stores. Capt. Peacock and the three companies of Royal Fusileers under his command, remain here; Col. Patterson and his battalion to go to Camden.

Thursday, 15th. Got in motion at twelve o'clock at night, and marched twelve miles to Saluda Ferry; crossed the river and halted.

Friday, 16th. Got in motion at half after four o'clock in the morning, and marched seven miles to the blacksmith's, and halted.

Saturday, 17th. Lay still in the field at the blacksmith's, or High Hill creek.

Sunday, 18th. Got in motion at two o'clock in the morning, and marched fourteen miles to a Capt. Wright's, of Col. Innes' regiment.

Monday, 19th. Got in motion at four o'clock in the morning, and marched to Cook's place, fourteen miles. This Cook is a Rebel Justice and Captain—a great persecutor of friends to Government. He is ordered down to John's Island, a place pointed out for the reception of such infamous villains.

Tuesday, 20th. Got in motion and marched to Davenport's, fourteen miles. He was formerly Captain of militia under Government. He has the name of a Tory from his neighbors; but many of his actions were doubtful.

Wednesday, 21st. Lay encamped at Davenport's, Little river.

Thursday, 22d. Got in motion at twelve, and marched ten miles to the fording place, Saluda river; crossed the men and baggage in a scow, and forded the horses; continued our march six miles to Ninety Six, where we halted. It is a village or country town—contains about twelve dwelling houses, a court-house and a jail, in which are confined about forty Rebels, brought in prisoners by the friends to Government, who have just now got the opportunity, and gladly embrace it, many of them having been obliged before this to hide in swamps to keep from prison themselves.   Ninety Six is situated on an eminence, the land cleared for a mile around it, in a flourishing part of the country, supplied with very good water, enjoys a free, open air, and is esteemed a healthy place. Here were condemned seventy-five friends to Government at one court ; five were executed—the others got reprieved.

Friday, 23d.   Lay in the field at Ninety Six.   Some friends came in, four were wounded.   The militia had embodied at Tuckasegie, on the South Fork of Catawba river—were attacked by a party of Rebels, under command of Gen. Rutherford.   The miltia were scant of ammunition, which obliged them to retreat.   They were obliged to swim the river at a mill dam.   The Rebels fired on them and killed thirty.*   Col. Ferguson, with forty American Volunteers, pushed with all speed in pursuit of the Rebels.   It is seventy miles distance from Ninety Six.   The militia are flocking to him from all parts of the country.

Saturday, 24th.   Took quarters in town, opposite the jail, where I have the constant view of the Rebels peeping through the grates, which affords some satisfaction to see them suffer for their folly.   Some of them are magistrates ; one the executioner of the five that were hanged here some time in April, 1779.

Sunday, 25th, to Tuesday, 27th.   Spent in cleaning, parade, and in the town.

Thursday, 29th, and Friday, 30th.   Still at Ninety Six.   Nothing extra.

Saturday, July 1st.   Took a ride into the country for exercise.

Sunday, 2d, to Saturday, 8th.   Still at Ninety Six.

Sunday, 9th.   The American Volunteers moved from Ninety Six at seven o'clock in the evening, under the command of Captain DePeyster, and marched seven miles to Island Ford, of Saluda river, on our way to meet a party of Rebels that were making approaches towards our lines. Dr. Johnson and I being late before we left our old quarters, without any guide, got out of the road ; found our mistake at a mill, three miles from the road we ought to have taken.   It turned out to be no great loss, as we have supplied ourselves with a grist of corn for our horses.   We came up to the detachment at one o'clock in the morning.   Our baggage had not arrived, which put us to the necessity of going to a house to lodge.   We found two women, and spent the night, though not to our satisfaction.   It afforded some merry scenes with those two modest country women.

---

*Col. Moore's defeat at Ramsour's Mill, June 20th.

Monday, 10th. Got in motion at five o'clock in the morning; crossed Saluda in a flat; marched nine miles to a Rebel Col. Williams' plantation, where we halted. Mrs. Williams and the children were at home, and were treated with the utmost civility. Col. Williams is with the Rebels, and is a very violent, persecuting scoundrel.

Tuesday, 11th. Got in motion at five o'clock in the morning, and marched eight miles to Indian creek, and halted during the heat of the day at one Ryan's, who is a good friend, and suffered much for his loyalty. Got in motion at six o'clock in the evening, and marched eleven miles to Duncan's creek, where we halted at a Widow Brown's.

Wednesday, 12th. Got in motion at five o'clock in the evening, and forded Duncan's creek and Enoree river. Continued marching to Capt. Frost's, at Padget creek, eight miles from the Widow Brown's. This evening met an express with the disagreeable news of a party of ours consisting of seventeen of the Legion, eighteen York Volunteers, and twenty-five militia being defeated at Col. Bratton's, at Fishing creek.*

Thursday, 13th. Lieut. Hunt of the Legion Cavalry came to our quarters at Capt. Frost's. He was one of the party defeated the twelfth inst. He gave an imperfect account of the affair. Capt. Huck commanded the party consisting of one subaltern and seventeen dragoons of the Legion, three subalterns and eighteen New York Volunteers, twenty-five militia men. They were sent in pursuit of a Rebel party, and arrived at twelve o'clock, Tuesday night, the 11th instant, at Col. Bratton's, at Fishing creek, and were very much fatigued. They thought to rest themselves. Unfortunately a Rebel party commanded by a Col. Lacey came upon them at four o'clock in the morning of the 12th, who were in amongst them, and had possession of every pass before they where apprised of it—except a road leading towards North Carolina, where Captain Huck, with four dragoons, attempted to make off. Huck got shot through the neck, of which he died. Mr. Hunt, with one dragoon, took a foot path leading to a swamp. The militia he could give no account of. We left Capt. Frost's about six o'clock in the evening; forded Tyger river, continued our march twelve miles to Sugar creek. Here we found two hundred militia encamped at Wofford's old field, Fair Forest, under command of Majors Plummer and Gibbs. The Rebels, we hear, are collecting in force at the Catawba Nation and Broad river.

Friday, 14th. Lay encamped at Fair Forest. Every hour news from different parts of the country of Rebel parties doing mischief. Light Infantry of Gen. Browne's corps joined us at twelve o'clock at night.

Saturday, 15th. Went in company with Capt. F. De Peyster, Dr. Johnson, and Lieut. Fletcher, to dine with Col. Fletchall. After dinner went to see his mill, which was a curiosity, having never seen such an one

---

* Capt. Hook or Huck defeated that morning.

before. The water falls fourteen feet perpendicularly down into a tub, fixed with buckets; from this tub runs up a shaft through the stone, and turns, as the cog turns, a double-geared mill. Returning to camp were informed that Capt. Dunlap had been obliged to retreat from Prince's Fort. Capt. Dunlap made an attack upon the Rebels; drove them from their ground, took one prisoner, who informed him that the Rebels were four hundred strong. Upon this information Dunlap thought proper to retreat, as his number was only fourteen American Volunteers and sixty militia. We lost two killed, a sergeant and private wounded, and one prisoner. The loss of the Rebels is uncertain—reports are, twenty or thirty killed. Upon this news arriving, Capt. De Peyster ordered the American Volunteers and militia to get in motion to support Dunlap. Capt. Frederick De Peyster, with one hundred militia men, marched twelve miles to McElwain's creek, where they met Dunlap.

Sunday, 16th. Dunlap with the men under his command marched down to Stephen White's plantation, where the American Volunteers and militia lay.

Monday, 17th. Lay at White's. The militia brought in four prisoners, one lad of fifteen years old, badly wounded in the arms.

Tuesday, 18th. Still at Mitchell's creek. This day Col. Ferguson came to us from Nintey Six; brought news that the Light Infantry were on their march to join us.

Wednesday, 19th. Still at White's plantation, on Mitchell's creek.

Thursday, 20th. Got in motion at five o'clock in the evening, and marched six miles to Fair Forest Ford, where we halted and lay all night.

Friday, 21st. Col. Balfour, with the Light Infantry from Ninety Six, joined us—we still remained at the Ford.

Saturday, 22d. The Light Infantry, American Volunteers, and three hundred militia, got in motion at seven o'clock in the evening; made a forced march of twenty-five miles to Lawson's Fork to surprise a party of Rebels, who, we were informed, lay there. We arrived at James Wood's plantation at six o'clock in the morning; greatly disappointed at finding no Rebels here. We were informed they were at Green river—twenty-five miles farther.

Sunday, 23d. Got in motion at one o'clock in the morning, and countermarched to our old ground, Fair Forest Ford.

Monday, 24th. Very much fatigued; slept all day.

Tuesday, 25th. Col. Balfour with the Light Infantry got in motion at two o'clock in the morning, and marched towards Ninety Six.

Wednesday, 26th. Lay at our old ground, Fair Forest.

Thursday, 27th. Got in motion at nine o'clock in the morning; forded Fair Forest river; marched about three miles and took up our ground in the wood.

Friday, 28th. Got in motion at seven o'clock in the morning, and marched eight miles to Col. Henderson's plantation, Pacolet river. Henderson is prisoner at Charlestown; he has a pretty plantation, with near two hundred acres of Indian corn growing.

Saturday, 29th. Got in motion at eight o'clock in the morning, and marched five miles to Thicketty river and halted; one of the soldiers killed a Continental rattle-snake, with thirteen rattles on.

Sunday, 30th. Got in motion at three o'clock in the morning; countermarched twelve miles to Armstrong's creek, Fair Forest. This day came into camp express from Anderson's fort, a Capt. Cook, aged sixty years, who has buried four wives, and now has his fifth on her last legs.

Monday, 31st. Got in motion at six o'clock in the morning, and marched ten miles to Mitchell's creek, Fair Forest; a very wet, disagreeable day; got thoroughly soaked.

Tuesday, August 1st. Lay at Mitchell's creek. Had intelligence that the Rebels had attacked Col. Turnbull at Rocky Mount, on Sunday the 30th; but could not learn the particulars.

Wednesday, 2d. Got in motion at four o'clock in the morning; marched four miles to Tyger river; forded that stream and continued our march to Capt. Bobo's, and halted. Had intelligence that Col. Turnbull beat off the Rebels; Capt. Hulett got wounded in the head. The Rebels were commanded by Gen. Sumter. He sent in a flag, demanding the post—Rocky Mount. Col. Turnbull sent word that he might come and take it. Sumter endeavored to do so, but was obliged soon to retreat with considerable loss. Col. Turnbull took two prisoners, who had previously been in his camp, drew ammunition, and then joined the Rebels, and were heard to say when firing, "take back your ammunition again." They were both hanged as a reward for their treachery.

Thursday, 3d. Lay at Bobo's; nothing extra.

Friday, 4th. Still at Bobo's. At six o'clock in the evening moved three-quarters of a mile for advantage of ground.

Saturday, 5th. Lay in the woods near Bobo's. Had intelligence that Fort Anderson, in which we had a Sergeant of the American Volunteers, and eighty militia men, was summoned on Sunday the 30th July, and given up in a dastardly manner, without exchanging a single shot.*

Sunday, 6th. Got in motion at seven o'clock in the evening. Left the heights near Bobo's, upon hearing that the Rebels were collecting in force at Ford's Mills. We made a forced march of sixteen miles in order to surprise them; marched all night; got to our ground at Jemmie's creek at six o'clock in the morning of the 7th, where we heard the Rebels had moved seven miles to Phillip's Ford.

---

* Col. Patrick Moore, commanding, taken by Col. Shelby and others.

Monday, 7th. Got in motion at seven in the evening, and made another forced march for them; and fording Jemmie's creek and the South and North branches of Tyger river. Got to the ground the Rebels were encamped on, at four o'clock on Tuesday morning, August eighth. They had intelligence of our move, and were likewise alarmed by the firing of a gun in our ranks; they sneaked from their ground about half an hour before we arrived.

Tuesday, 8th. Learning that the Rebel wagons were three miles in front of us at Cedar Springs, Captain Dunlap, with fourteen mounted men, and a hundred and thirty militia, were dispatched to take the wagons. He met three Rebels coming to reconnoitre our camp; he pursued, took two of them—the other escaped, giving the Rebels the alarm. In pursuit of this man, Dunlap and his party rushed into the centre of the Rebel camp, where they lay in ambush, before he was aware of their presence. A skirmish ensued, in which Dunlap got slightly wounded, and had between twenty and thirty killed and wounded— Ensign McFarland and one private taken prisoners. The Rebel loss is uncertain. A Maj. Smith, Capt. Potts, and two privates, were left dead on the field. Col. Clarke, Johnson [Robertson,] and twenty privates were seen wounded. We pursued them five miles to the Iron Works, but were not able to overtake them, they being all mounted. We countermarched five miles to Cedar Springs, and halted to refresh during the heat of the day. At six in the evening, marched and took a height near the ground the Rebels left.

Wednesday, 9th. Lay on the heights; nothing extra.

Thursday, 10th. Sent the wounded to Musgrove's Mills, Enoree river, to be attended by Dr. Ross. We marched about seven miles to Culbertson's plantation, on Fair Forest. Express arrived from Col. Turnbull at Rocky Mount, with orders to join him. By the express heard that Sumter had attacked Hanging Rock the 6th instant. The North Carolinians were first attacked; they gave way. Brown's corps came up, but were obliged to give way. The Legion Cavalry came in the Rebels' rear, and soon gained the day. Brown's corps suffered much—three officers killed, and three wounded—an hundred men taken prisoners.

Friday 11th. Got in motion at six o'clock in the morning. Marched ten miles to Maj. Gibbs' plantation; lay all night.

Saturday, 12th. Got in motion at seven o'clock in the morning, and marched seven miles to a Rebel Capt. Stripling's plantation. He has taken protection, and as yet has not broken his promise. A Maj. Rutherford* came with a flag; in consequence of his coming in our rear, without giving signal by drum or trumpet, was detained all night, and threatened with imprisonment.

---

*Maj. Rutherford, a son of Gen. Rutherford, distinguished himself at Ramsour's Mill, and was subsequently killed at Eutaw Springs.

Sunday, 13th. Got in motion at five o'clock in the morning, and marched nine miles to Tinker creek. At seven in the evening got in motion and marched five miles to Smith's Mills, on Swift's creek. Here we lay all night.

Monday, 14th. Got in motion at four o'clock in the morning; Marched to the Quaker fording place; forded Tyger river, continued our march to a Rebel Col. James Lisle's plantation. Lisle is in the Rebel service—his family at home.

Tuesday, 15th. Got in motion at seven o'clock in the morning. Marched two miles to Lisle's Ford; forded Broad river—proceeded seven miles to a Mr. Coleman's in Mobley's settlement; halted during the heat of the day. Got in motion at seven o'clock in the evening; marched two miles to the camp of the New York Volunteers, where we got intelligence that Gen. Gates lay within three miles of Camden, with an army of seven thousand men. Col. Turnbull had orders the twelfth to retreat from Rocky Mount, and act as he saw proper—to get to Camden if he could. Sumter appeared with cannon at Rocky Mount, about twelve hours after Col. Turnbull left it, in order to make a second trial for the post. He found not so harsh a reception as his first attempt.

Wednesday, 16th. Got in motion at seven o'clock in the morning, and marched two miles to Mobley's meeting house for convenience of ground.

Thursday, 17th. Got in motion at nine o'clock in the morning, and marched six miles to a Rebel Col. Winn's plantation. Winn is at James Island, a prisoner.

Friday, 18th. Lay at Winn's plantation, waiting news from Camden, having spies out upon every quarter.

Saturday, 19th. Lay at Winn's plantation. An express arrived from Camden with the agreeable news of Lord Cornwallis' attacking and totally defeating Gates' army on the morning of the 16th; twelve hundred were killed and wounded, left on the field; and one thousand prisoners, eight brass field pieces taken, being all the Rebels had in the field, several stand of colors, all their ammunition wagons, a hundred and fifty wagons of baggage, provisions, and stores of different kinds. All this with the trifling loss on our side of not more than ten officers killed and wounded, and two or three hundred non-commissioned officers and privates. We received orders to pursue Sumter, he having the only remains of what the Rebels can call a corps in these parts at present. At six o'clock in the evening our wagons were ordered forward that we might pursue Sumter with vigor. At seven we got in motion. That very moment an express arrived from Col. Innes', who was on his way from Ninety Six to join us, informing us that he had been attacked by a body of Rebels at Musgrove's Mills on Enoree river; that himself, and Major Fraser of his regiment, were wounded, as were Capt. Peter Campbell, Lieuts. Chew and Camp, of Col. Allen's regiment. He wished for support as many of the militia had left him. This, to our great mortification, altered the course of our march. At eleven at night, we got in motion ; marched all night ; forded Broad river at sun-rising.

Sunday, 20th. Proceeded four miles, and took up our ground at Peter's creek, where we lay all day, fatigued with our night's march, being eighteen miles. While we lay at Col. Winn's, a Mr. Smith was executed for joining the Rebels after he had taken protection, and been allowed to embody himself with our militia.

Monday, 21st. Got in motion at one o'clock in the morning, and marched six miles to a Rebel Capt. Lipham's on Padget creek. Took up our ground at five o'clock in the morning. This morning was so cold that we were glad to hover round large fires as soon as we halted. About one o'clock a Mr. Duncan came to our camp with the agreeable news that Col. Tarleton, with three companies of the Light Infantry, and the Legion Cavalry, fell in with Sumter about twelve o'clock on Saturday, the nineteenth.* He found them all asleep after the fatigue of two nights' rapid retreat. Their horses were all at pasture. The first alarm was the Light Infantry firing upon them. Col. Tarleton, with his usual success, gained a complete victory over Gen. Sumter ; took two brass field pieces, made two hundred and fifty prisoners, eight hundred horses, thirty wagons, and retook a hundred of Brown's men that were captured at Hanging Rock. Captain Duncan made his escape from the Rebels during the engagement, he being a prisoner Got in motion at eleven o'clock in the evening ; marched ten miles to Tyger river ; forded it at break of day.

Tuesday morning, 22d. Continued our march four miles to Harrison's plantation, on Fair Forest, where we halted.

Wednesday, 23d. Got in motion at six o'clock in the morning, and marched six miles to John Blasingame's plantation, on Sugar creek, where we took up our ground. Col. Ferguson set out for Camden.

Thursday, 24th. Still lay at Blasingame's, on Sugar creek.

Friday, 25th. Still at Blasingame's.

Saturday, 26th. Got in motion at six o'clock in the morning; marched six miles to John Wofford's plantation, on McClure's creek.

Sunday, 27th. Lay at McClure's creek ; nothing extra.

Monday, 28th. Got in motion at five o'clock, and marched six miles to Culbertson's plantation, near Fair Forest river.

Tuesday, 29th, to Thursday, 31st. Lay at Culbertson's ; nothing extra.

Friday, September 1st. Still remained at Culbertson's. Maj. Ferguson joined us again from Camden with the disagreeable news that we

---

*It was really the preceding day, Friday, 18th.

were to be separated from the army, and act on the frontiers with the militia.

Saturday, 2d.   Got in motion at eleven o'clock in the morning; forded Fair Forest river, and marched ten miles to the Iron Works, on Lawson's Fork of Pacolet river.   Here was a Rebel militia-man that got wounded in the right arm at the skirmish at Cedar Springs, the eighth of August.   The bone was very much shattered.   It was taken off by one Frost, a blacksmith, with a shoemaker's knife and carpenter's saw.   He stopped the blood with the fungus of the oak, without taking up a blood vessel.

Sunday, 3d.   My friend Johnson and I bathed in the stream at the Iron Works.

Monday, 4th.   Got in motion at six o'clock in the morning, and marched ten miles to Case's creek, where we halted all night.

Tuesday, 5th.   Got in motion at five o'clock in the evening, and marched a mile and a half to Pacolet river, and halted.   The fresh was so high we could not ford the river.   I took lodging, with my friend Johnson, who was very unwell, at one Coleman's, who is a very warm Tory.   His wife and all her children have been stripped of all their clothes, bedding, and other furniture.   She was mother of five children in two years.

Wednesday, 6th.   Got in motion at eight o'clock in the morning ; marched six miles to Buck's creek ; dined at one Nelson's.   Here was a hearty old man, named William Case, a hundred and nine years old.   He is a native of New England.   Talks very strong ; gives some faint description of New England.   His memory began to fail seven years past ; he lost his eyesight about eighteen months past ; is otherwise very hale ; walks amazingly spry, and danced a jig.

Thursday, 7th.   Got in motion at seven o'clock in the morning; crossed Buck creek, and the division line of South and North Carolina ; marched six miles farther, and halted.   Maj. Ferguson, with about fifty of the American Volunteers, and three hundred militia, got in motion at six o'clock in the evening, and marched to Gilbert Town in order to surprise a party of Rebels that we heard were there.   Capt. DePeyster and I remained on the ground we took in the morning, with the remainder of the American Volunteers and militia.

Friday, 8th.   Got in motion at eight in the morning, and marched six miles to Broad river, and took a height where we halted, and waited orders from Maj. Ferguson.

Saturday, 9th.   Remained on the ground ; received intelligence from Maj. Ferguson to keep our post.   He was returning to keep a good lookout, as the Georgians were coming towards us.

Sunday, 10th.   Col. Ferguson joined us about eleven o'clock at night.

Monday, 11th.   Got in motion at four o'clock in the evening; forded

Broad river and continued on our march ten miles to one Adair's plantation, and halted.

Tuesday, 12th. Maj. Ferguson, with forty American Volunteers and one hundred militia, got in motion at two o'clock in the morning, and marched fourteen miles through the mountains to the head of Cane creek, in Burke County, in order to surprise a party of Rebels we heard lay there. Unfortunately for us, they had by some means got intelligence of our coming, in consequence of which, Mr. McDowell, with three hundred infamous villains like himself, thought it highly necessary to remove their quarters. However, we were lucky enough to take a different route from what they expected, and met them on their way, and to appearance one would have thought they meant sincerely to fight us, as they drew up on an eminence for action. On our approach they fired and gave way. We totally routed them, killed one private, wounded a Capt. White, took seventeen prisoners, twelve horses, all their ammunition, which was only twenty pounds of powder, after which we marched to their encampment, and found it abandoned by those Congress heroes. Our loss was two wounded and one killed. Among the wounded was Capt. Dunlap, who received two slight wounds. After the skirmish we returned to one Allen's to refresh ourselves. We got in motion about four o'clock in the afternoon, and countermarched about six miles to a Rebel Mr. Jones', where we halted all night.

Wednesday, 13th. Got in motion about eight o'clock in the morning and continued countermarching to a Rebel Col. Walker's plantation where we met Capt. Ryerson and Lieut. Fletcher with the remainder of the American Volunteers and militia. Here we took up our ground, very much fatigued with our enterprise.

Thursday, 14th. Lay still at Col. Walker's. The poor, deluded people of this Province begin to be sensible of their error, and come in very fast. Maj. Ferguson, with thirty American Volunteers, and three hundred militia, got in motion at six o'clock, and marched to the head of Cane creek, and halted at one Wilson's.

Friday, 15th. Capt. DePeyster and I, who remained at Col. Walker's with the remainder of the American Volunteers and militia, got in motion at six o'clock in the morning, and marched twelve miles to one Bowman's, near the head of Cane creek, and halted. This creek is so amazingly crooked that we were obliged to cross it nineteen times in marching four miles. Mrs. Bowman is an exceedingly obliging woman. She had a child about four years old, who had smoked tobacco almost three years. At four o'clock in the afternoon got in motion, and marched a mile and a half to Wilson's, where we joined Maj. Ferguson. At ten o'clock in the evening we got in motion, with the American Volunteers and five hundred militia, leaving Capt. Ryerson and Lieut. Fletcher, with two hundred militia, to guard the baggage, and marched fifteen miles to one John Forsyth's, on the banks of the Catawba, to surprise Col. McDowell. We arrived there about six o'clock in the morning of the 16th. Col. McDowell had left this place the 14th. We countermarched to one Devore's, and halted to refresh ourselves. At three o'clock got in motion ; marched to Pleasant Garden Ford, Catawba river ; forded it, and continued our march to one George Cathy's plantation, about a mile and a half from Devore's. Pleasant Garden is a very handsome place. I was surprised to see so beautiful a tract of land in the mountains. This settlement is composed of the most violent Rebels I ever saw, particularly the young ladies.

Sunday, 17th. Got in motion and marched two miles to Buck's creek, forded it, and continued our march two miles farther to a Rebel Maj. Davidson's plantation, and halted.

Monday, 18th. Got in motion, countermarched to Buck creek, forded it, and proceeded on five miles to Richey's Ford, on Catawba river, forded it, and marched to a Rebel Alexander Thompson's plantation, six miles farther, and halted.

Tuesday, 19th. Got in motion at five o'clock in the morning, and marched about eleven miles to a Rebel Mr. Hemphill's plantation, and halted. At seven o'clock in the evening, I went about a mile and joined Capt. Ryerson and the militia under his command.

Wednesday, 20th. Got in motion at six o'clock in the morning, and marched a mile and a half to one White's plantation, where we joined Maj. Ferguson again. This day three officers belonging to Cruger and Allen's regiments, joined us from Ninety Six, with fifty militia men.

Thursday, 21st. Got in motion at five o'clock in the morning and marched fourteen miles to a Rebel Samuel Andrew's plantation, and halted. On the march I saw eight wild turkeys.

Friday, 22d. Got in motion at five o'clock in the morning ; marched five miles to Col. Walker's plantation, and halted.

Saturday, 23d. Got in motion at nine o'clock in the morning ; marched three miles to Gilbert Town ; took up our ground on a height about half a mile from the town. This town contains one dwelling house, one barn, a blacksmith's shop, and some out-houses.

Sunday, 24th. Five hundred subjects came in, also a number of ladies. Received intelligence from Col. Cruger, that he had marched from Ninety Six to Augusta, to the assistance of Col. Browne, who was besieged by six hundred Rebels, under the command of Col. Clarke. Fortunately for Col. Browne, the Cherokee Indians, for whom he is agent, were coming to Augusta for their yearly presents. They met the Rebels just as they were going into the town, which obliged them to fight. The Rebels being too numerous, and the Indians unacquainted with field fighting, were obliged to make the best of their way to a fort on one flank of the town, where Col. Browne had retired to. He made a very gallant defence for five days, two of which he was without bread or water. On Col. Cruger's approach, the Rebels moved off with their plunder, of which they had a tolerable share. Col. Cruger arrived time enough to retake the cannon which they had taken from Browne, and about thirty prisoners.

Monday, 25th, and Tuesday, 26th. Lay at Gilbert Town; nothing extra.

Wednesday, 27th. Got in motion at five o'clock in the morning, and marched three miles to Rucker's Mill, and halted.

Thursday, 28th. Got in motion at five o'clock in the morning; marched seven miles to Mountain creek, forded it, although very difficult, continued on about a mile farther to Twitty's Ford of Broad river, and took up our ground on its banks. At six o'clock in the evening got in motion, forded the river; marched two miles to McDaniel's Ford of Green river; forded it, and marched two miles farther; halted on the road; lay on our arms till four o'clock the next morning.

Friday, 29th. We then, at that early hour, moved on three miles to one James Step's plantation, and halted. This man has been very unfortunate in his family; his wife, who is a very decent woman, was caught by the Indians about a twelvemonth past. They scalped and tomahawked her several times in the head, treated the infant she had in her arms in a most inhuman and savage manner. They mashed its head in such a manner that its recovery is truly astonishing; but what this poor, unhappy woman seems most to regret is the loss of her oldest son, whom the savages took, and she now remains in a state of uncertainty, not having heard from him since.

Saturday, 30th. Lay at James Step's with an expectation of intercepting Col. Clarke on his return to the mountains; but he was prudent enough to take another route.

Sunday, October 1st. Got in motion at five o'clock in the morning, and marched twelve miles to Denard's Ford of Broad river, and took up our old ground where we lay the 8th September.

Monday, 2d. Got in motion at four o'clock in the afternoon; forded Broad river; marched four miles; formed in line of action and lay on our arms. This night I had nothing but the canopy of heaven to cover me.

Tuesday, 3d. Got in motion at four o'clock in the morning; marched six miles to Camp's Ford of Second Broad river, forded it and continued on six miles to one Armstrong's plantation, on the banks of Sandy Run. Halted to refresh; at four o'clock got in motion; forded Sandy Run; marched seven miles to Buffalo creek; forded it; marched a mile farther and halted near one Tate's plantation. John West came in camp, who is a hundred and one years of age; is amazingly strong in every sense.

Friday, 6th. Got in motion at four o'clock in the morning, and marched sixteen miles to Little King's Mountain, where we took up our ground.

Saturday, 7th. About two o'clock in the afternoon twenty-five hundred Rebels, under the command of Brig.-Gen. Williams, and ten Colonels, attacked us. Maj. Ferguson had eight hundred men. The action continued an hour and five minutes; but their numbers enabled them to surround us. The North Carolina regiment seeing this, and numbers being out of ammunition, gave way, which naturally threw the rest of the militia into confusion. Our poor little detachment, which consisted of only seventy men when we marched to the field of action, were all killed and wounded but twenty; and those brave fellows were soon crowded as close as possible by the militia. Capt. DePeyster, on whom the command devolved, saw it impossible to form six men together; thought it necessary to surrender to save the lives of the brave men who were left. We lost in this action, Maj. Ferguson, of the Seventy-first regiment, a man much attached to his King and country, well informed in the art of war; he was brave and humane, and an agreeable companion; in short, he was universally esteemed in the army, and I have every reason to regret his unhappy fate. We had eighteen men killed on the spot; Capt. Ryerson and thirty-two privates wounded of Maj. Ferguson's detachment; Lieut. McGinnis, of Allen's regiment of Skinner's Brigade, killed. Taken prisoners, Two Captains, four Lieutenants, three Ensigns, and one Surgeon, and fifty-four sergeants rank and file, including the mounted men under the command of Lieut. Taylor. Of the militia, one hundred were killed, including officers; wounded, ninety; taken prisoners, about six hundred. Our baggage all taken, of course. Rebels lost Brig.-Gen. Williams, one hundred and thirty-five, including officers, killed; wounded, equal to ours.

Sunday, 8th. They thought it necessary to move us sixteen miles, to one Waldron's plantation, where they halted.

Monday, 9th. Moved two miles and a half to Bullock creek; * forded it, and halted on the banks.

Tuesday, 10th. Moved twenty miles and halted in the woods.

Wednesday. 11th. Moved at eight o'clock in the morning; marched twelve miles to Col. Walker's, and halted.

Thursday, 12th. Those villains divided our baggage, although they had promised on their word we should have it all.

Friday, 13th. Moved six miles to Bickerstaff's plantation. In the evening their liberality extended so far as to send five old shirts to nine of us, as a change of linen—other things in like proportion.

Saturday, 14th. Twelve field officers were chosen to try the militia

---

* Apparently Boren's creek —Bullock's creek was some fifteen or eighteen miles distant.

prisoners—particularly those who had the most influence in the country. They condemed thirty—in the evening they began to execute Lieut.-Col. Mills, Capt. Wilson, Capt. Chitwood, and six others, who unfortunately fell a sacrifice to their infamous mock jury. Mills, Wilson, and Chitwood died like Romans—the others were reprieved.

Sunday, 15th. Moved at five o'clock in the morning. Marched all day through the rain—a verv disagreeable road. We got to Catawba, and forded it at Island Ford, about ten o'clock at night. Our march was thirty-two miles. All the men were worn out with fatigue and fasting—the prisoners having no bread or meat for two days before. We officers were allowed to go to Col. McDowell's, where we lodged comfortably. About one hundred prisoners made their escape on this march.

Monday, 16th. Moved at two o'clock in the afternoon. Marched five miles; forded the north branch of Catawba and John's river; halted at a Tory plantation.

Tuesday, 17th. Moved at eight o'clock in the morning. Marched fifteen miles; halted at Capt. Hatt's plantation. Three prisoners attempted to make their escape this night; two succeeded—the other was shot through the body.

Wednesday, 18th. About five o'clock in the morning the Rebels executed the man who unfortunately got wounded in attempting to make his escape. We moved at eight o'clock in the morning, and marched eighteen miles to Moravian creek, and halted.

Thursday, 19th. Moved at eight o'clock in the morning; forded Moravian creek, passed by Wilkes Court House, and marched sixteen miles to one Hagwoods' plantation, and halted.

Friday, 20th. Moved at eleven o'clock in the morning; marched six miles to Mr. Sale's plantation, and halted.

Saturday, 21st. Several Tory women brought us butter, milk, honey, and many other necessaries of life. Moved at ten o'clock in the morning, and marched fourteen miles to Mr. Headpeth's plantation, a great Tory, who is at present with Lord Cornwallis. We lodged at Mr. Edward Clinton's, who is likewise with Lord Cornwallis.

Sunday, 22d. Moved at ten o'clock in the morning. Obtained liberty to go forward with Col. Shelby to Salem, a town inhabited by Moravians. Rode ten miles, and forded Yadkin river at Shallow Ford. Proceeded on fourteen miles farther to Salem. Went to meeting in the evening; highly entertained with the decency of those people, and with their music. Salem contains about twenty houses, and a place of worship. The people of this town are all mechanics; those of the other two Moravian settlements are all farmers, and all stanch friends to Government.

Monday, 23d. Lay at Salem in the evening. Two Continental

officers slept at the tavern, on their way to join their army, One Mr. Simons, a Lieutenant of Col. Washington's dragoons, was exceeding polite, pitied our misfortune in falling into the hands of their militia.

Tuesday, 24th. Moved at ten o'clock in the morning ; marched six miles to the old town called Bethabara. Here we joined the camp again. This town is about as large as the other; but not so regularly laid out. The inhabitants very kind to all the prisoners. This night Dr. Johnson and I were disturbed by a Capt. Campbell, who came into our room, and ordered us up in a most peremptory manner. He wanted our bed. I was obliged to go to Col. Campbell, and wake him to get the ruffian turned out of the room ; otherwise he would have murdered us, having his sword drawn, and strutting about with it in a truly cowardly manner.

Wednesday, 25th. The men of our detachment, on Capt. DePeyster passing his word for their good behavior, were permitted to go into houses in the town without a guard.

Thursday, 26th, to Saturday, 28th. Nothing extra.

Sunday, 29th. Col. Cleveland waited on Capt. DePeyster and the rest of the officers, and asked us if we, with our men, would come and hear a sermon at ten o'clock. He marched the militia prisoners from their encampment to the town, and halted them ; and sent an officer to our quarters to acquaint us they were waiting for us. We then ordered our men to fall in ; marched to the front of the prisoners ; the whole then proceeded on to a height about half a mile from the town. Here we heard a Presbyterian sermon, truly adapted to their principles and the times ; or, rather, stuffed as full of Republicanism as their camp is of horse thieves.

Monday, 30th. A number of the inhabitants assembled at Bethabara to see a poor Tory prisoner executed for a crime of the following nature, viz : A Rebel soldier was passing the guard where the prisoners were confined, and like a brute addressed himself to those poor unhappy people in this style : " Ah, d—n you, you'll all be hanged." This man, with the spirit of a British subject, answered, "Never mind that, it will be your turn next." But Col. Cleveland's goodness extended so far as to reprieve him.

Tuesday, 30th. Rode to Salem in company with Capt. DePeyster, Dr. Johnson and Mr. Supple. This night very cold ; froze ice a quarter of an inch thick—the first this fall.

Wednesday, November 1st. My friend, Dr. Johnson, insulted and beaten by Col. Cleveland for attempting to dress a man whom they had cut on the march. Col. Armstrong relieved Cleveland in the afternoon, and took the command.

Thursday, 2d. Took a walk with Capt. DePeyster, Dr. Johnson and Mr. Taylor to Bathania, three miles from Bethabara. This town contains about thirty houses ; it is regularly laid out.

Friday, 3d. Heard by a countryman, who was moving his family over the mountains to Nolachucky, that General Leslie had landed at James river, in Virginia.

Saturday, 4th. Dined at a country house.

Sunday, 5th. Set off from Bethabara in company with Lieut. Taylor, Lieut. Stevenson, and William Gist, a militia-man, about six o'clock in the evening. We marched fifteen miles to Yadkin river; forded it, found it very disagreeable. We continued on twenty miles farther to Mr. Miller's plantation, an exceeding good subject. Here we arrived just at daybreak the next morning.

Monday, 6th. Took up our ground in the bushes, about half a mile from the house. At ten o'clock, we sent Mr. Gist to the house for some victuals. He found Mr. Miller at home, who very readily gave us all the assistance that lay in his power. About two o'clock, he brought us some victuals, which we were very happy to see, being very hungry after our fatiguing march the night before. In conversation, which very naturally run upon the safest way, guides, etc., Mr. Miller told us he knew a militia Capt. Turner, and one or two more subjects, then lying in the bushes, who would be very happy to join Lord Cornwallis; and they were also excellent guides. On this we consulted, and thought it prudent to stay all night. Mr. Miller then fetched us a blanket, and immediately set out to find those people.

Tuesday, 7th. Mr. Miller returned informing us that one of those men would be with us at six o'clock in the evening. We waited till seven, but the man not coming, we thought it prudent to go without him. We set out about half after seven; marched six miles to one Carpenter's. When we arrived there, Mr. Carpenter advised us to remain there the remainder of the night, and he would go to Mr. Miller, and send him again for the men. We then consulted, and thought it best to stay a day or two—then to proceed on, without a guide.

Wednesday, 8th. Lay very snug in the bushes. About four o'clock in the afternoon, Mr. Carpenter returned and told us Mr. Miller was gone in search of a guide, and was to return with an answer as soon as possible. Suffered exceedingly with the cold this day.

Thursday, 9th. Heard of the Rebels following us, but they getting false intelligence, returned again, which was much in our favor. In the course of the day, we thought it would be prudent to get the best directions we could, and proceed on, without a guide, rather than remain too long in one place, lest some of those people might be treacherous. We got direction from Mr. Carpenter for sixty miles, and at six o'clock in the evening, set out; marched thirty miles, and halted in the woods at daybreak.

Friday, 10th. Suffered very much with the cold. At six o'clock in the evening set out again. This night saw the moon in an eclipse, and heard several wolves bark. Passed a Rebel party consisting of twelve or fourteen, who lay about twenty yards from the road by a fire; but

33

very fortunately for us, they were all asleep. We marched thirty miles and arrived at Colbert Blair's, just at daybreak.

Saturday, 11th. It began to rain just after we got to Mr. Blair's. Lucky we were indeed. This good man secreted us in his fodder-house, and gave us the best his house afforded.

Sunday, 12th. Remained at Mr. Blair's ; a rainy, disagreeable day.

Monday, 13th. Set out from this good man's fodder-house. He conducted us about three miles to a Mr. F. Rider's, who guided us seven miles farther, over the Brushy Mountains, to Catawba river. Mr. John Murray, who lived on the bank of the river, put us over in a canoe, and conducted us three miles to Mr. Ballou's. This old man was about sixty years of age ; but his love for his King and his subjects induced him to get up, although very late at night, and guided us seven miles to a Mr. Hilterbrine's. On the way the old man informed us he had two sons who lay out in the woods, who were anxious to go to our army, and were also good guides. He also told us of one Williams, that was a good guide, and who would be glad to go with us. We told the old man we should be very happy to have them, as the road began to grow more dangerous, and we quite unacquainted with the way. This poor old man expressed a great deal of anxiety for our safety, and at last told us he would go the next day and endeavor to find them, and send them to us. We arrived at Hilterbrine's about six o'clock in the morning of the 14th. He received us with great caution, lest we should be treacherous ; but when he found we were British officers he was very kind.

Wednesday, 15th. Just as we were drinking a dish of coffee, on a rock, after dusk, those three young men came to us on horseback, which made us very happy. We set out immediately, and marched twenty miles over the Brushy Mountains, where there was nothing but Indian paths. Crossed several small rivers. We arrived at one Sheppard's plantation, just at daybreak of the 16th. This poor family were so completely stripped of everything they had, by the Rebels, that they could give us nothing but a hoe cake, and some dried beef, which was but a very indifferent repast for hungry stomachs. At six o'clock in the evening set out ; marched sixteen miles to Camp's Ford of Second Broad river ; forded it, and continued on three and a half miles farther to Island Ford of Main Broad river ; forded it, and marched one mile to Capt. Townsend's plantation. This man received three balls in the action on King's Mountain, and was at home on parole. He was very happy to see us, and gave us the best his house afforded.

Friday, 17th. Set out at six o'clock in the evening ; marched twelve miles to a Mr. Morris'. Here we were told that a party of Rebels were directly in our front ; that we had better remain there that night, in which time we could send Mr. Williams, who was with us, and well acquainted with that neighborhood, to get a militia Capt. Robins, who lay out in the woods, and was going to our army in a day or two. This man was so good a guide that it induced us to stay.

Saturday, 18th. Lay in the woods ; fared pretty well.

Sunday, 19th. Mr. Williams returned, but without effecting what he went after. We had a council of safety ; found it necessary to proceed on. We got Mr. Murray to guide us to the main road that leads to the Iron Works, which is twelve miles distant. We set out about three o'clock in the afternoon ; took by-paths. and got in the main road just at dusk. We crossed Pacolet river, Lawson's Fork, and Tyger river ; passed a Rebel guard ; marched thirty-seven miles, and arrived at James Duncan's plantation, half an hour before daybreak of the 20th. About ten o'clock Mrs. Duncan rode out to see if she could get any intelligence of our army, and of the Rebel army, that we might shun the latter. Mrs. Duncan returned in less than an hour, with the disagreeable news that the Rebel army was marching within two miles of us, and were going to encamp at Blackstock's, about four miles from us. This news truly discouraged me. About five o'clock in the evening Mr. Duncan came to us with agreeable news—that Col. Tarleton was in pursuit of the Rebels. At six o'clock a Mr. Jackson came to us, and informed us he had seen Col. Tarleton ; he had also heard he had had an action with Sumter, who commanded the Rebels, but did not know the particulars. He advised us to go to his house and stay all night, as we would be perfectly safe there, and the next morning go to Mr. Smith's, where we could hear the particulars of the action, as there were some of the Legion wounded there. We agreed to what the man said ; staid all night at his house, where we were treated very kindly.

Tuesday, 21st. Mr. Duncan conducted us to Mr. Smith's, where we found six of the Legion wounded.

Wednesday, 22d. Set out from Archey Smith's on horseback, which the subjects in that neighborhood supplied us with. They brought us on thirteen miles to one Adair's. Here we dismounted, and those good people returned. We continued thirteen miles to Williams' Fort, which was commanded by Col. Kirkland, who received us very kindly.

Thursday, 23d. Set out from Col. Kirkland's, who was kind enough to lend us horses as far as Saluda. Left the horses here ; crossed in a scow ; walked a mile to Col. Mayson's : dined ; got horses and rode to Ninety Six. Arrived at Capt. John Barbarie's * quarters, about eight o'clock in the evening.

Friday, 24th. Remained at Ninety Six ; nothing extra.

Saturday, 25th. Set out for Charleston, Where I arrived the 29th of November ; nothing worth notice on the journey.

---

*Capt. Barbarie belonged to the New Jersey Volunteers; was captured at Staten Island in 1777; doubtless shared in the siege of Charleston, as he did in the siege of Ninety Six, during which he was wounded ; and was again wounded at Eutaw Springs. He received half pay, and settled at St. Johns, New Brunswick, where he became a Colonel of the militia, and a magistrate. He died at Sussex Vale in 1818 at the age of sixty-seven. His son, Andrew Barbarie, was a member of the Assembly of that Province.